NELSON COUNTY PUBLIC LIBRARY

3 7080 1023 9227 0

FEB 2 2 2018

MAKING TINY TOYS in Wood

Ornaments & Collectible Heirloom Accents

745.592   37080102392270
Clem   Clements, Howard.
           Making tiny toys in
           wood

NELSON CO. PUBLIC LIBRARY
201 Cathedral Manor
Bardstown, KY 40004-1205

A Scroll Saw Woodworking & Crafts book

FOX CHAPEL
PUBLISHING

D1225367

DEDICATION
To my daughter, Laura.

ACKNOWLEDGMENTS
Photography: Mike Mihalo
Test cutting and step photos: Rolf Beuttenmuller
Patterns: Carolyn Mosher
Assembly drawings: Frank Rohrbach

© 2017 by Howard Clements and Fox Chapel Publishing Company, Inc., 903 Square Street, Mount Joy, PA 17552.

Making Tiny Toys in Wood is an original work, first published in 2017 by Fox Chapel Publishing Company, Inc. The patterns contained herein are copyrighted by the author. Readers may make copies of these patterns for personal use. The patterns themselves, however, are not to be duplicated for resale or distribution under any circumstances. Any such copying is a violation of copyright law.

ISBN 978-1-56523-915-9

To learn more about the other great books from Fox Chapel Publishing, or to find a retailer near you,
call toll-free 800-457-9112 or visit us at *www.FoxChapelPublishing.com*.

Printed in Singapore
First printing

Because working with wood and other materials inherently includes the risk of injury and damage, this book cannot guarantee that creating the projects in this book is safe for everyone. For this reason, this book is sold without warranties or guarantees of any kind, expressed or implied, and the publisher and the author disclaim any liability for any injuries, losses, or damages caused in any way by the content of this book or the reader's use of the tools needed to complete the projects presented here. The publisher and the author urge all readers to thoroughly review each project and to understand the use of all tools before beginning any project.

INTRODUCTION

When my first grandson was born, I decided to make an ornament for each year. I made the twenty-second one in 2016. I have enjoyed designing and building an original ornament every year.

I have expanded my gift list for others besides my grandchildren and a few friends. I am an avid hunter, and I give each landowner where I hunt an ornament each year as well. The response I receive is overwhelming. I hope each of you will enjoy building these ornaments as much as I did.

You can do most of the work on a scroll saw and drill press. Some pieces are quite small, so please be very careful! You can find most of the thin pieces of wood at craft stores, supply houses, or online. A thickness sander does an excellent job when crafting thin pieces of wood. If you make very many of these ornaments, it would be wise to purchase one of these machines.

Have fun, and good luck with all of your projects!

CONTENTS

24 Golf Cart

26 Windmill

28 Tractor

36 Ferris Wheel

38 Bread Truck

40 Wishing Well

18 Noah's Ark

20 Carousel

22 Locomotive

30 Wagon

32 Tugboat

34 1909 Cadillac

42 Barn

44 Horseless Carriage

MATERIALS

WOOD

Toy ornaments are perfect projects for using up your scrap wood. The pieces you'll need are small, most of them are thin, and you can mix and match colors. I use a combination of basswood and assorted hardwoods, but you can also use good quality plywood, such as Baltic birch—just be aware that the striped edges will show unless you paint them. I use a thickness sander to make sure the wood fits together well.

GLUE

You'll need a bottle of good quality wood glue, such as Elmer's® Wood Glue, Titebond®, or Gorilla® Wood Glue. This type of glue is made to bond wood, and it will create a tight bond if you apply it according to the manufacturer's instructions, clamp or weight the pieces, and let it dry thoroughly. I don't recommend using tacky glue, because it doesn't create as strong a bond. Similarly, cyanoacrylate (CA) glue, such as Super Glue®, dries fast but also lacks the strength of wood glue.

Be sure to clean up any glue squeeze-out before it dries so it doesn't ruin the final finish.

PAINT

You are welcome to paint as much or as little of the toy ornaments as you like. As you'll see from the photos, I only painted accents on most of mine because I like to let the natural colors of the wood show. When I do paint the ornaments, I use inexpensive craft acrylic paints.

If you paint any pieces before you assemble an ornament, keep the paint away from the gluing surfaces to ensure a tight bond later.

FINISH

I finish my ornaments in a couple of different ways. I might dunk them in Danish oil or boiled linseed oil to highlight the wood grain or simply spray them with a light coat of clear lacquer or acrylic finish. Sometimes I even leave them unfinished.

TOOLS

SCROLL SAW & BLADES

You can cut all of the pieces for these projects using just a scroll saw. (I haven't tried it, but I think you could cut most of them with a coping saw, as well.) You'll need a selection of blades ranging from #2/0 to #5; use the smaller (lower number) blades for thinner wood and the larger (higher number) blades for the thicker wood. Reverse-tooth blades will reduce the roughness of the cut on the reverse side of the wood. Buy plenty of blades and change them often. For additional scrolling tips, see Scroll Saw Basics on page 8.

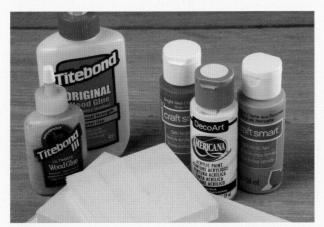

You'll need a handful of common materials to make these ornaments—scraps of wood, glue, sandpaper, and maybe a few toy wheels.

These projects are perfect for people just getting started in woodworking because you don't need many tools.

DRILL & BITS

I use a drill press to ensure my holes are perfectly vertical, but you could also use a hand drill. You'll need a set of small bits; many of the holes are ⅛" (3mm) or smaller. I often use a #43 wire-size bit, which is commonly used for electronics and machining. Although you may not find them at a large home-improvement store, a local hardware store should carry wire-size bits, or you can order them online. Dowels and toothpicks vary in diameter, so you may have to experiment in scrap to make sure the holes you drill match the piece of wood you're working with.

CLAMPS

To get a good glue joint, you'll need to clamp the pieces. Rubber bands and binder clips (from an office supply store) make good clamps for small pieces. Harbor Freight also sells inexpensive lightweight clamps.

SCROLL SAW BASICS

Here are a few tips to help making scrolling a little easier.

SQUARING THE TABLE

Most scroll saws have an adjustable table that allows you to make cuts at different angles. There are times when you want the saw set at an angle, but you'll do most cutting with the blade perpendicular to the table. If the table is even slightly off square, the cuts will be angled, which can interfere with the way the pieces fit together.

The most common method for squaring a table uses a small metal square, or right-angle tool. Set the square flat on the saw table against a tensioned blade. Adjust the table to form a 90° angle to the blade.

Other Useful Materials

Toy wheels
Dowel scraps and round wooden toothpicks
Sandpaper
Screw eyes

The cutting-through method is also popular. Saw through a piece of scrap wood at least ¾" (1.9cm) thick and check the angle of the cut using a square. Adjust the table until you get a perfectly square cut.

You can also use the kerf-test method. Take a 1¾" (4.4cm)-thick piece of scrap wood and cut about ½" (1.3cm) into it. Stop the saw, back the blade out, and spin the wood around to the back of the blade. If the blade slips easily into the kerf, the table is square. If it doesn't slide into the kerf, adjust the table and perform the test again until the blade slips in easily.

ATTACHING PATTERNS

Temporary-bond spray adhesive is the most common method used to attach patterns to stock. Cover the wood blank with blue painter's tape to lubricate the blade and make the pattern easier to remove. Photocopy the pattern. Spray the adhesive on the back of the copy of the pattern, wait a few seconds, and then press the pattern onto the taped blank. Rubber cement or glue sticks work similarly.

Some scrollers prefer to use clear adhesive shelf paper. Place a piece onto the table, shiny side up. Cut the pattern pieces apart if necessary, apply spray adhesive to the back, and attach the patterns to the shelf paper. Cut the pattern pieces out. To apply them to the blanks, peel the liner off the back of the shelf paper.

STACK CUTTING

Stack cutting lets you cut several pieces of a project—or even several projects—at one time. Essentially, you attach several blanks together and cut them as one unit. One way to attach blanks is with tape. Align all of the layers and wrap a layer of tape around the outside edge. You can also wrap the whole stack in tape for extra stability. Use masking tape, painter's tape, or clear packaging tape. Hot-melt glue is another option. Glue the blanks together with a dot of hot-melt glue on each side. You can also join pieces by driving brads or small nails into as many waste areas as you can. Cut off any overhanging nails as close to the surface as you can, and then sand them flush to avoid scratching or catching on the table.

BLADE TENSION

Before inserting a blade, completely remove the tension. Clamp both ends of the blade into the blade holders and adjust the tension. Push on the blade

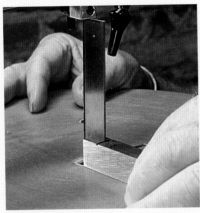
Squaring the table

Kerf test squaring

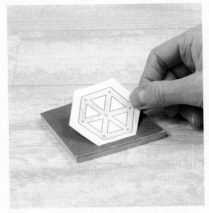
Pattern on tape

Hot glue stacking

Tape stacking

Blade entry hole

with your finger. It should flex no more than 1/8" (3mm) forward, backward, or side to side.

A blade that does not have enough tension will wander. It will also flex from side to side, making for irregular or angled cuts. If you press too hard on a loose blade, it will usually snap. A blade that has too much tension is more susceptible to breaking and tends to pull out of the blade holders. In general, it is better to make the blade too tight than too loose.

BLADE-ENTRY HOLES

If you need to cut a piece from the center of a blank without cutting in from the side, you'll need a blade-entry hole. Place the hole near a cutting line to prolong the blade life, but don't place the hole on a curving line or inside corner (if possible). Drill a vertical hole. Use a drill press if you have one; otherwise, use a hand drill and make the holes as vertical as possible. Drill through the blank into scrap wood to prevent tear out on the back side of the blank. If you have the

space, use a larger bit—it will make it easier to thread the blade through the wood.

REMOVING PATTERNS

A quick wipe of mineral spirits will remove most adhesives left behind on the wood. Commercial adhesive removers work as well.

PHOTOCOPYING PATTERNS

Some photocopy machines may cause a slight distortion in the copies, so it is important to use the same photocopier for all of the pieces of a project and to photocopy the patterns in the same direction. Distortion is more likely to occur on very large patterns.

CHOOSING A BLADE

- Use larger blades (higher numbers) as the thickness or the density (hardness) of the wood increases. A rule of thumb is to use a #5 or #7 blade for

¾" (1.9cm) to 1" (2.5cm)-thick medium-hard wood (such as cherry, walnut, or maple).

- Use smaller blades (#3 and smaller) for thin wood. These blades cut more slowly, which gives you additional control when cutting thin wood. Choose a blade that will allow you to cut the smallest turns and details without breaking every few cuts.
- If you are stack cutting, choose a blade based on the thickness of the stack. If you cut eight ⅛" (3mm)-thick blanks at once (giving you an effective thickness of 1", or 2.5cm), use a #5 or #7 blade. If you're cutting four ⅛" (3mm)-thick blanks, use a #2 or #3 blade.
- Consider the intricacy of the cuts. Larger blades will not cut tight corners or fit into small holes. When cutting intricate projects, choose the smallest blade that will cut the thickness of wood.

Safety Tips for Scrollers

- Use glasses, goggles, or similar equipment to protect your eyes.
- Remove any loose clothing or jewelry before you operate the saw. If you have long hair, tie it back.
- Work in a well-ventilated area. Consider using a mask, an air cleaner, a dust collector, or any combination of these to protect your lungs from fine dust.
- Be sure that the work area is well lighted.
- Keep your hands a safe distance away from the blade.
- Don't work when you are tired or unfocused.

Troubleshooting

Simple solutions to common scrolling problems.

- **You're not sure which end of the blade is the top.** If you're using a crown-tooth blade, it isn't important because these blades cut in either direction. For all other blades, the majority of the teeth should point down. Determine the tooth direction by running your thumbnail along the middle of the blade. It catches more in the direction the teeth are pointing, and it feels rougher if you run your finger in that direction, almost like coarse sandpaper. Once you determine the blade direction on one blade, use a dab of cheap red nail polish to mark the top ends of the other blades in that pack.
- **The blades keep breaking.** First, check the tension. If the blade is too tight and you press too hard while sawing, the blade can break. However, if the blade is too loose, it can catch in the wood as it flexes from side to side and break as well. Remember, tight is good, but too tight is bad.

  If the tension seems right but the blades are still breaking, try a larger blade. See "Choosing a Blade" for tips on matching the blade to the wood.

  Blades also break because they heat up, lose their temper, and become fragile. Friction created during the cutting process heats blades, so lubricate the blade by applying a little beeswax to it or by covering the blanks with tape (the lubricant that keeps the tape from sticking to itself will also lubricate the blade).

  Finally, dull blades break more easily. The easiest ways to tell that the blade is getting dull are that

you need to push harder for the blade to cut or you notice that the saw is cutting more slowly. This is a gradual process, so you may not realize the blade is dull until it breaks. If you do notice slowing or difficulty pushing, replace the blade. It is normal to use several blades per project; large projects or those made from thick or dense wood will require even more blades.

- **The blade pops out of the blade holders, or the tension won't hold.** Manufacturers coat blades in light oil to keep them from rusting during transit. The oil is one of the top reasons a blade slips. Keep a scrap of sandpaper near the saw and rub both ends of the blade with it before installing the blade in the saw to remove the oil. Blades also slip because the set screws that hold them in place are polished smooth over time by the action of the blade and stop gripping. A bit of sandpaper will also remove this polish and give the screws a better grip.
- **The wood is scorching.** Dull blades cause friction. All cutting dulls the blade, but cutting dense wood accelerates the process. Scorched wood is a good indication that the blade is getting dull and should be replaced. A resinous wood, such as cherry, will always burn if you don't lubricate the blade with tape or wax. Very hard wood, such as hickory, will dull blades quickly and cause scorching. Finally, sawdust packed into the cut will cause scorching. Try using a skip-tooth blade, which removes the sawdust as it cuts.

MAKING A BULLDOZER

I'm going to lead you step-by-step through the process to build one toy—the bulldozer. Once you see how I make that project, you'll be able to use similar methods to make the others.

Materials
- Scrap wood:
  - ⅜" (10mm) thick
  - ¼" (6mm) thick
  - ⅛" (3mm) thick
  - 1⁄16" (2mm) thick
- Dowel: 3⁄16" (5mm) dia.
- Toothpicks: round wooden
- Wire: scrap (optional; see Step 12)
- Screw eye: ⅛" (3mm)

- Tape, hot glue, or wire brads for stacking (see page 8)
- Painter's tape and spray adhesive for attaching patterns
- Wood glue
- Sandpaper
- Finish: See page 7 for suggestions

Tools
- Scroll saw and blades
- Drill and bits: #43 wire bit (or size to match toothpicks and dowels)
- Clamps

GETTING STARTED

Marking Holes

Use an awl to mark the center of every hole. This ensures the holes are placed correctly, especially in small pieces.

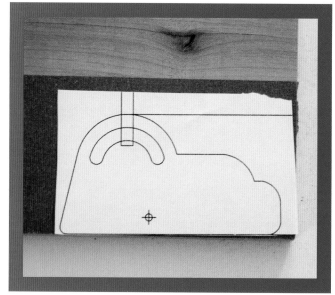

STEP 1: Photocopy the pattern and loosely cut out the separate pieces. Cover the wood blanks with blue painter's tape, marking the grain on the tape as needed for reference. Spray adhesive on the backs of the patterns and attach them to the taped wood, aligning the grain as appropriate.

CUTTING THE PIECES

STEP 2: Cut the perimeter of the chassis (A). Match a drill bit to your toothpick or dowel (I used a #43), clamp the chassis in a vise, and drill a hole in the top of the chassis for the exhaust pipe (K). Then, drill a blade-entry hole and cut the opening that surrounds the exhaust pipe. Drill the pivot hole through the chassis.

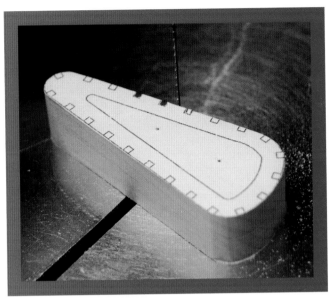

STEP 3: Stack the two track blanks (B) with tape, glue, or fine nails in the center waste area (see "Stack Cutting" on page 8). Cut the perimeters of the tracks. Cut very shallow notches approximately ¹⁄₁₆" (2mm) wide for the treads; two cuts placed right next to each other works well. Then, drill a blade-entry hole, cut the center of the track, and separate the stack.

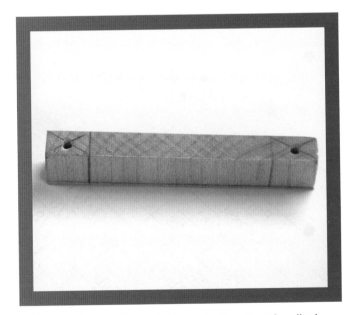

STEP 4: Cut the pivot blocks (G). To make it easier to handle the small pieces, cut a long piece, mark and drill the holes, and then cut them to size. Match a drill bit to your blade pin toothpick or dowel before you drill the holes (I used a #43 wire size).

STEP 5: Cut the blade arms (C). Make both arms at once by stacking and securing the blanks and cutting them as one (see "Stack Cutting" on page 8). Using the drill bit you chose in Step 4, drill the holes in the arms while the pieces are still taped together. Because the arms will pivot, you may have to go up a drill size. Cut the blade (D).

CUTTING THE PIECES (CONTINUED)

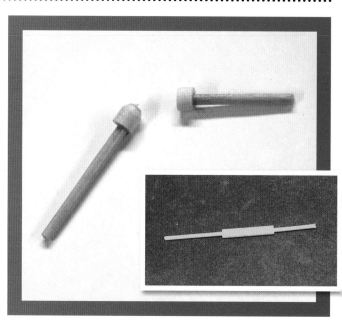

STEP 6: Cut the cab. Stack the pieces for the cab bottom (E) and cab top (F) (see "Stack Cutting" on page 8) using the notched bottom pattern. Match a drill bit to your toothpicks or dowels (I used a #43). Drill the support holes through the thinner cab bottom but do not drill through the thicker cab top piece. Separate the stack and cut the notch in the cab bottom piece.

STEP 7: Make the pivot pins. Cut a 2" (5.1cm)-long piece of ³⁄₁₆" (5mm) dowel (I). Match a drill bit to a toothpick (I used a #43 bit) and drill a ¼" (6mm)-deep hole in each end of the dowel. Glue a toothpick (J) into each end. Then, cut a ⅛" (3mm) length of dowel from each end to form two pins. Lightly sand all of the cut pieces.

ASSEMBLING THE BULLDOZER

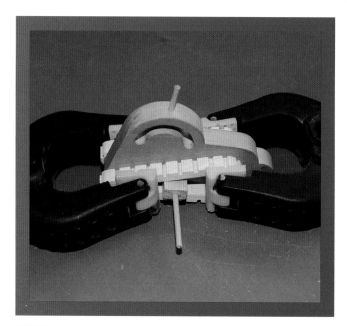

STEP 8: Glue the tracks (B) and pivot blocks (G) to the chassis (A). Align the pivot blocks with a toothpick and fit the tracks around them. Place a ⅛" (3mm)-thick shim under the chassis to create a small gap under the chassis (the tracks should rest on the bench). Glue and clamp the tracks and blocks in place, and then remove the toothpick. Cut the exhaust pipe (K) to length, round the end, and glue it in place.the toothpick. Cut the exhaust pipe (K) to length, round the end, and glue it in place.

STEP 9: Assemble the cab. Cut four toothpicks or dowels to length (H) and glue them into the cab bottom (E) piece. While the glue is still wet, fit and glue the top (F) in place.

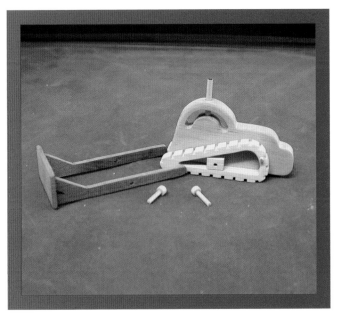

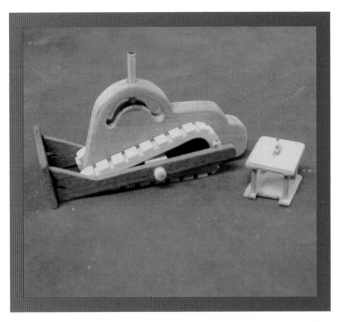

STEP 10: Clamp (but don't glue) the blade arms (C) to the tracks (B). Center the blade (D) on the arms and glue it in place.

STEP 11: Align the blade arms (C) and test-fit the pivot pins (I, J). Cut the pins to length and glue them to the pivot blocks. Don't get glue on the blade arms or they won't pivot. Glue the cab assembly to the top of the chassis with the notch forward.

STEP 12: Complete the project. If desired, drill a very small hole and glue a scrap of toothpick or wire into one track to keep the blade arms from swinging up too far. Drill a pilot hole and add a screw eye to the cab for hanging the ornament. Finish as desired (see page 7 for suggestions).

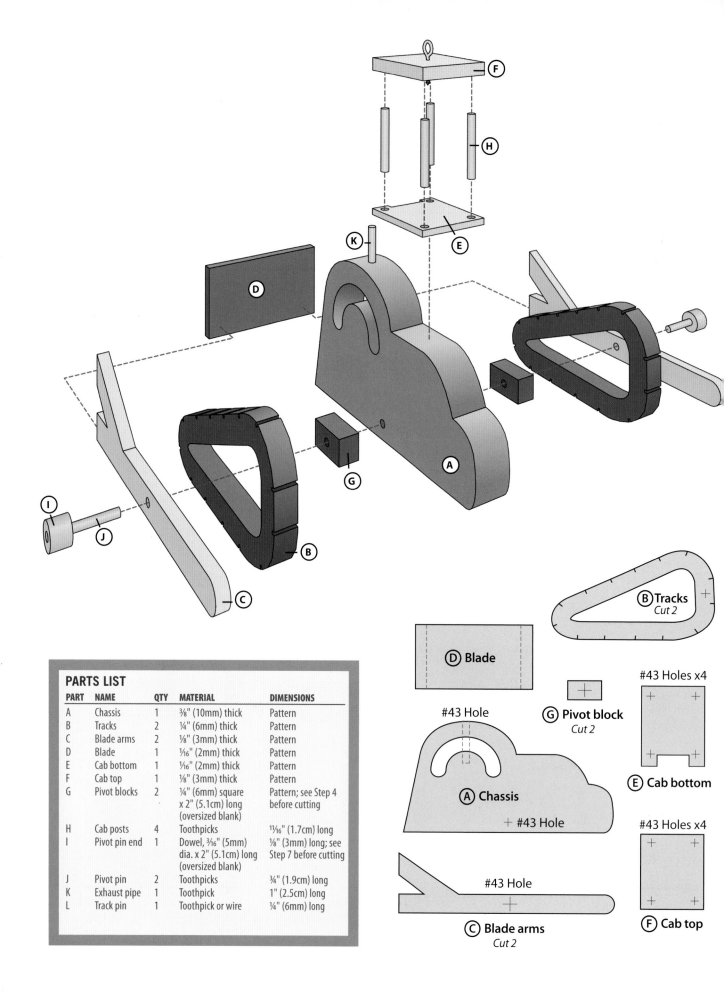

PARTS LIST

PART	NAME	QTY	MATERIAL	DIMENSIONS
A	Chassis	1	⅜" (10mm) thick	Pattern
B	Tracks	2	¼" (6mm) thick	Pattern
C	Blade arms	2	⅛" (3mm) thick	Pattern
D	Blade	1	1⁄16" (2mm) thick	Pattern
E	Cab bottom	1	1⁄16" (2mm) thick	Pattern
F	Cab top	1	⅛" (3mm) thick	Pattern
G	Pivot blocks	2	¼" (6mm) square x 2" (5.1cm) long (oversized blank)	Pattern; see Step 4 before cutting
H	Cab posts	4	Toothpicks	11⁄16" (1.7cm) long
I	Pivot pin end	1	Dowel, 3⁄16" (5mm) dia. x 2" (5.1cm) long (oversized blank)	⅛" (3mm) long; see Step 7 before cutting
J	Pivot pin	2	Toothpicks	¾" (1.9cm) long
K	Exhaust pipe	1	Toothpick	1" (2.5cm) long
L	Track pin	1	Toothpick or wire	¼" (6mm) long

B Tracks *Cut 2*

D Blade

#43 Hole

G Pivot block *Cut 2*

#43 Holes x4

E Cab bottom

A Chassis
+ #43 Hole
+ #43 Hole

#43 Hole

C Blade arms *Cut 2*

#43 Holes x4

F Cab top

CHAPTER 3:
PATTERNS

NOAH'S ARK

Materials
- Scrap wood:
  ¾" (1.9cm) thick
  ⅝" (1.6cm) thick
  ⅛" (3mm) thick
- Screw eye: ⅛" (3mm)
- Tape, hot glue, or wire brads for stacking (see page 8)
- Painter's tape and spray adhesive for attaching patterns
- Wood glue
- Sandpaper
- Acrylic paint
- Permanent marker: black
- Finish: See page 7 for suggestions

Tools
- Scroll saw and blades
- Drill and bits
- Clamps

CONSTRUCTION NOTES

1. The ark is made of stacked layers. You'll need one copy of the layers A-B pattern and three copies of the layers C-D-E pattern. Trim the layers C, D, and E patterns to form three differently sized patterns, attach each to thin wood, and cut the pieces. Attach the layer A pattern to its blank, drill a blade-entry hole, and cut the center. Glue it to layer B and cut the perimeter of the stacked piece. Glue all of the layers together.

2. Cut the cabin (G), and then draw or paint the door. To cut the roof (F), attach the pattern to the wood, tilt the left side of the saw down 25°, and then cut the four sides. Paint the roof, glue it to the cabin, and glue the cabin to the hull.

3. Cut and paint Noah (H) and the animals (I). Let them dry, and then glue them to the ark as desired. Drill a small pilot hole and attach a screw eye to the top.

PARTS LIST

PART	NAME	QTY	MATERIAL	DIMENSIONS	PART	NAME	QTY	MATERIAL	DIMENSIONS
A	Ark layer	1	⅛" (3mm) thick	Pattern	F	Ark roof	1	¾" (1.9cm) thick	Pattern
B	Ark layer	1	⅛" (3mm) thick	Pattern	G	Ark cabin	1	⅝" (1.6cm) thick	Pattern
C	Ark layer	1	⅛" (3mm) thick	Pattern	H	Noah	1	⅛" (3mm) thick	Pattern
D	Ark layer	1	⅛" (3mm) thick	Pattern	I	Animals	2 each	⅛" (3mm) thick	Pattern
E	Ark layer	1	⅛" (3mm) thick	Pattern					

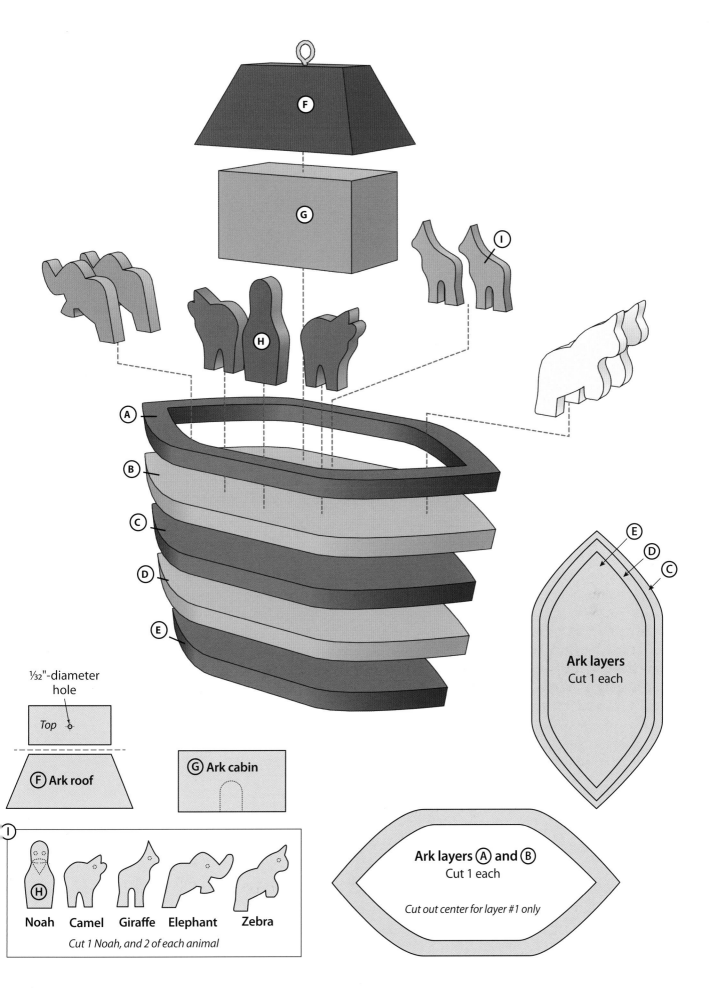

F

G

I

A

B

C

D

E

H

E
D
C

Ark layers
Cut 1 each

1/32"-diameter
hole

Top

F Ark roof

G Ark cabin

Ark layers A and B
Cut 1 each

Cut out center for layer #1 only

H

Noah Camel Giraffe Elephant Zebra
Cut 1 Noah, and 2 of each animal

CAROUSEL

Materials

- Scrap wood:
  ¾" (1.9cm) thick
  ¼" (6mm) thick
  ⅛" (3mm) thick
- Dowel: ³⁄₁₆" (5mm) dia.
- Toothpicks: round wooden
- Acetate sheeting: scrap for shim
- Screw eye: ⅛" (3mm)

- Tape, hot glue, or wire brads for stacking (see page 8)
- Painter's tape and spray adhesive for attaching patterns
- Wood glue
- Sandpaper
- Acrylic paint
- Finish: See page 7 for suggestions

Tools

- Scroll saw and blades
- Drill and bits:
  ³⁄₁₆" (5mm) dia.; #43 or size to match toothpicks
- Clamps
- Lathe (optional)

CONSTRUCTION NOTES

1. Ensure the hole in the base (A) is perfectly vertical and that the center post (E) is vertical when you glue it in place. Stack the top and bottom (B) (see page 8 for instructions), drill the holes as marked, mark one corner so you can keep the pieces aligned, and cut the pieces.

2. To make the horses (D), cut an oversized blank, attach six patterns to the face, and drill toothpick-sized holes in the edge as marked on the patterns (see diagram). Then, cut the six horses, remove the patterns, and paint them as desired. Cut the horse posts (F) and glue the horses onto them in staggered positions. Glue the posts into the bottom. Cut a shim from a piece of plastic, such as acetate, cut or punch a hole in the center, and place it on the center post between the base and the bottom to allow for free movement. Slide the bottom onto the center post in the base, align the top, and glue it to the horse posts.

3. For the roof (C), cut the square blank and drill a hole in the center as marked. Then, either taper the sides using a lathe or compound-cut the piece into a pyramid and sand it as desired. (To compound cut, tape or draw the triangle-shaped pattern on two adjacent sides of the wood. Cut one side, tape the waste wood back in place, turn the blank, and cut the other side.) Dry-fit the roof onto the center post and ensure it clears the top by ¹⁄₁₆" (2mm); cut the center post if needed. Drill a pilot hole and add a ⅛" (3mm) screw eye to the roof for hanging.

PARTS LIST

PART	NAME	QTY	MATERIAL	DIMENSIONS
A	Base	1	¼" (6mm) thick	Pattern
B	Top & Bottom	2	⅛" (3mm) thick	Pattern
C	Roof	1	¾" (1.9cm) thick; 3" (7.6cm) square	Pattern; see Step 3 before cutting
D	Horses	6	⅛" (3mm) thick; ¾" x 8" (1.9cm x 20.3cm) (oversized blank)	Pattern; see Step 2 before cutting
E	Center post	1	³⁄₁₆" (5mm)-dia. dowel	3" (7.6cm) long
F	Horse posts	6	Toothpicks	1⅞" (4.8cm) long
G	Shim	1	Acetate sheeting/ thin plastic	Trace a quarter and punch a hole in the center

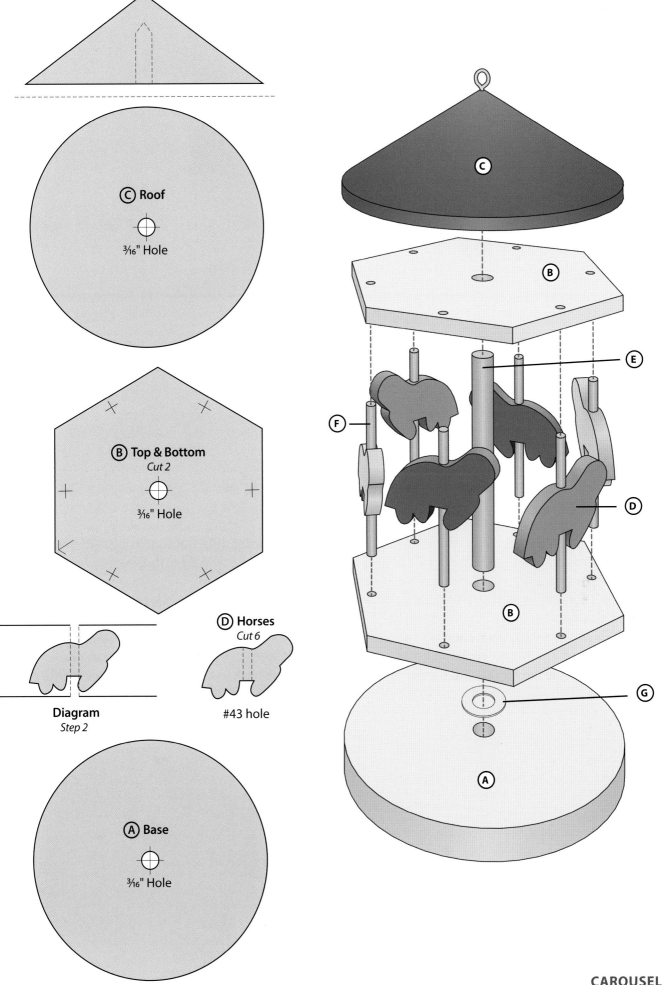

C Roof
3/16" Hole

B Top & Bottom
Cut 2
3/16" Hole

D Horses
Cut 6
#43 hole

Diagram
Step 2

A Base
3/16" Hole

LOCOMOTIVE

Materials

- Scrap wood:
  1⁹⁄₁₆" (3.9cm) thick
  ¼" (6mm) thick
  ³⁄₁₆" (5mm) thick
  ⅛" (3mm) thick
- Dowels:
  ¾" (1.9cm) dia.; ⅛" (3mm) dia.; ³⁄₁₆" (5mm) dia.
- Axle pegs: 2 each
  ³⁄₁₆" (5mm) dia.
- Wooden wheels: 4 each
  ½" (1.3cm) dia. (optional)
- Screw eye: ⅛" (3mm)
- Tape, hot glue, or wire brads for stack cutting (see page)
- Painter's tape and spray adhesive for attaching patterns
- Wood glue
- Sandpaper
- Finish: See page 7 for suggestions

Tools

- Scroll saw and blades
- Drill and bits: ⅛" (3mm); ⁹⁄₆₄" (3.5mm); ³⁄₁₆" (5mm); ¼" (6mm); ⁵⁄₁₆" (8mm)
- Clamps

CONSTRUCTION NOTES

1. Attach the patterns and cut the pieces, drilling holes as marked. Stack-cut and drill the rear wheels (G) so the holes align (see page 8 for instructions). Taper the front edges of the cow catcher (B). Flatten the bottom of the boiler (C).
2. Glue the cow catcher to the front of the chassis (A). Glue the boiler to the chassis. Glue the boiler blocks (D) to the chassis on each side of the boiler. Using a ⁹⁄₆₄" (3.5mm) bit, drill a hole into the center of one block, through the boiler, and out the other block. See the diagram.
3. Glue the cab (E) to the chassis, and glue the roof (F) to the cab. Drill a ¼" (6mm)-dia. hole in the chassis for the rear axle. Drill through the glue joint if necessary to ensure a good hole. Glue the rear axle (O) to one rear wheel (G), slide the axle through the chassis, align the other wheel so the crank holes are in the same position, and glue on the other rear wheel.
4. Glue one side of the piston block axle (J) into a piston block (I), using the ⅛" (3mm) hole. Slide the axle through the boiler and glue the other piston block to the opposite side. Place the cranks (H) into the piston blocks and attach them to the rear wheels with the crank pegs (K).
5. Glue one front wheel (M) to each front axle (N). Slide the axles through the holes in the front wheel block (L) and glue a second wheel to each axle. Glue the assembly to the bottom of the chassis. Drill a pilot hole and insert a ⅛" (3mm) screw eye in the center top of the boiler for hanging.

PARTS LIST

PART	NAME	QTY	MATERIAL	DIMENSIONS
A	Chassis	1	¼" (6mm) thick	Pattern; do not drill hole yet
B	Cow catcher	1	¼" (6mm) thick	Pattern
C	Boiler	1	¾" (1.9cm)-dia. dowel	1⅝" (4.1cm) long; flatten bottom
D	Boiler blocks	2	⅛" (3mm) thick	¼" wide x ¹³⁄₁₆" long (6mm x 2cm)
E	Cab	1	1⁹⁄₁₆" (3.9cm) thick	Pattern
F	Cab roof	1	⅛" (3mm) thick	1⅛" x 1⁵⁄₁₆" (2.9cm x 3.3cm)
G	Rear wheels	2	³⁄₁₆" (5mm) thick	Pattern
H	Cranks	2	⅛" (3mm) thick	Pattern
I	Piston blocks	2	¼" (6mm) thick	Pattern
J	Piston block axle	1	⅛" (3mm)-dia. dowel	1¾" (4.4cm) long
K	Crank pegs	2	³⁄₁₆" (5mm)-dia. axle peg	Cut shaft to ⁷⁄₁₆" (1.1cm) long
L	Front wheel block	1	¼" (6mm) thick	Pattern
M	Front wheels	4	⅛" (3mm) thick x ½" (1.3cm) dia.	Purchased OR Pattern
O	Rear axle	1	³⁄₁₆" (5mm)-dia. dowel	1¼" (3.2cm) long
N	Front axles	2	⅛" (3mm)-dia. dowel	1⁷⁄₁₆" (3.cm) long

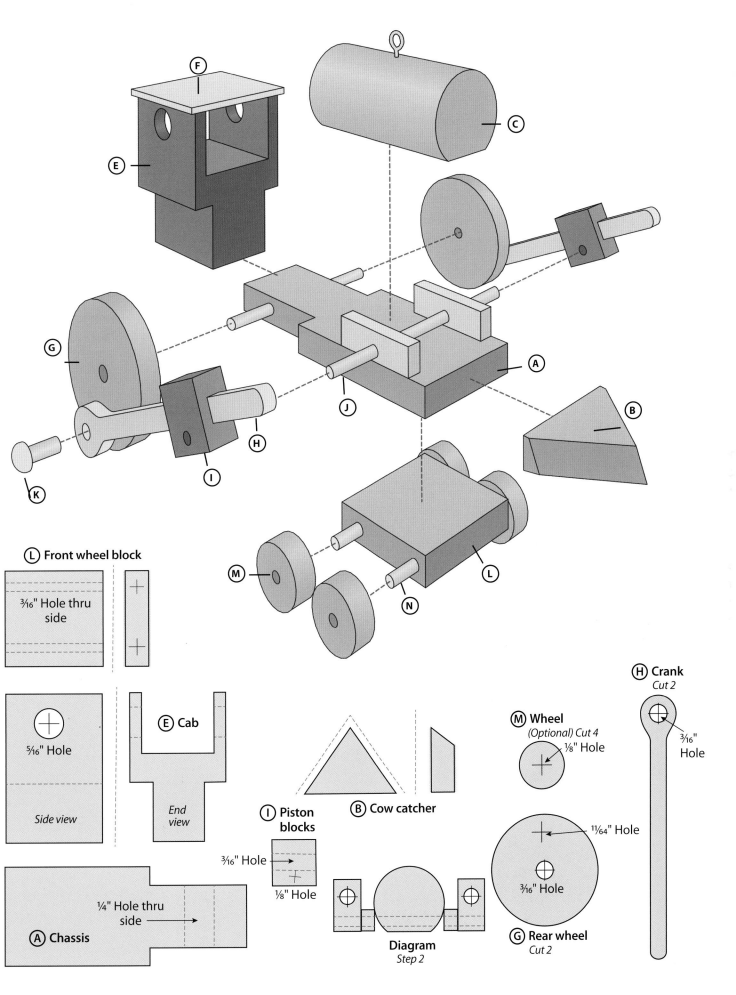

L Front wheel block

3/16" Hole thru side

E Cab

5/16" Hole

Side view

End view

B Cow catcher

I Piston blocks

3/16" Hole

1/8" Hole

Diagram
Step 2

M Wheel
(Optional) Cut 4
1/8" Hole

H Crank
Cut 2
3/16" Hole

11/64" Hole

3/16" Hole

G Rear wheel
Cut 2

1/4" Hole thru side

A Chassis

GOLF CART

Materials

- Scrap wood:
  13⁄16" (2cm) thick
  1⁄4" (6mm) thick
  3⁄16" (5mm) thick
  1⁄8" (3mm) thick
- Dowel: 1⁄8" (3mm)
  dia.; optional: scrap
  3⁄4" (1.9cm) dia.
- Toothpicks: round wooden
- Wooden wheels: 4 each
  3⁄4" (1.9cm) dia. (optional)

- Screw eye: 1⁄8" (3mm)
- Tape, hot glue, or wire
  brads for stacking (see
  page 8)
- Painter's tape and
  spray adhesive for
  attaching patterns
- Wood glue
- Sandpaper
- Finish: See page 7
  for suggestions

Tools

- Scroll saw and blades
- Drill and bits: #43 or sized
  to match toothpicks;
  9⁄64" (3.5mm); 1⁄4" (6mm)
- Clamps

CONSTRUCTION NOTES

1. Attach the patterns and cut the pieces. You can stack-cut the fenders (D, E) (see page 8 for instructions). Test the drill bit to be sure #43 works with your toothpicks and drill the holes as marked; do not drill the holes in the fenders yet.

2. Glue the hood (B) and the seat block (C) to the base (A). Glue the fenders onto the sides. Using a #43 bit, drill holes about halfway through fenders and glue in the canopy posts (G). Align the canopy (F) and drill its post holes, being careful not to drill all the way through; glue it to the posts.

3. Glue the seat (H) to the seat block. Glue the shaft (J) into the steering wheel (I) and glue the assembly into the hole in the hood. Glue one wheel (K) to each axle (L). Slide the axles through the holes in the base and glue a second wheel to each axle. Drill a pilot hole and insert a 1⁄8" (3mm) screw eye in the center top of the boiler for hanging.

4. Assemble two golf clubs and place them in the hole at the back of the golf cart.

PARTS LIST

PART	NAME	QTY	MATERIAL	DIMENSIONS
A	Base	1	1⁄4" (6mm) thick	13⁄16" x 3" (2cm x 7.6cm); see drawing for holes
B	Hood	1	13⁄16" (2cm) thick	Pattern
C	Seat block	1	13⁄16" (2cm) thick	Pattern
D	Front fenders	2	3⁄16" (5mm) thick	Pattern
E	Back fenders	2	3⁄16" (5mm) thick	Pattern
F	Canopy	1	1⁄8" (3mm) thick	15⁄16" x 21⁄4" (3.3cm x 5.7cm)
G	Canopy posts	4	Toothpicks	15⁄16" (3.3cm) long
H	Seat	1	13⁄16" (2cm) thick	Pattern
I	Steering wheel	1	1⁄4" (6mm) thick OR 3⁄4" (1.9cm)-dia. dowel	Use pattern on wood OR cut 1⁄4" (6mm) length of dowel
J	Steering wheel shaft	1	Toothpick	3⁄4" (1.9cm) long
K	Wheels	4	3⁄4" (1.9cm) dia.	Purchased
L	Axles	2	1⁄8" (3mm)-dia. dowel	11⁄4" (3.2cm) long
M	Golf club heads	2	1⁄4" (6mm) thick	Pattern
N	Golf club shafts	2	Toothpicks	1 11⁄16" (4.2cm) long

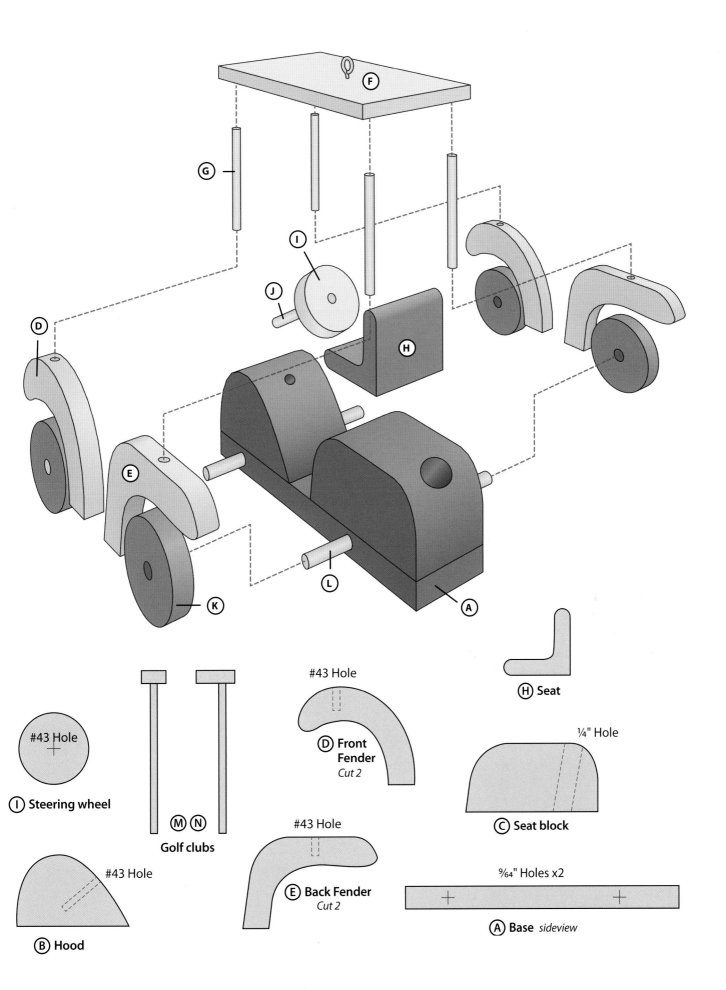

(F)

(G)

(I)

(J)

(D)

(E)

(H)

(K)

(L)

(A)

(H) Seat

#43 Hole

(D) Front
Fender
Cut 2

¼" Hole

(C) Seat block

#43 Hole

(I) Steering wheel

(M) (N)
Golf clubs

#43 Hole

(E) Back Fender
Cut 2

%4" Holes x2

(A) Base *sideview*

#43 Hole

(B) Hood

WINDMILL

Materials

- Scrap wood:
  1⅛" (2.9cm) thick
  ¾" (1.9cm) thick
  ¼" (6mm) thick
  ³⁄₁₆" (5mm) thick
  ¹⁄₁₆" (2mm) thick
- Toothpicks:
  round wooden
- 6d box nail
- Axle peg: ³⁄₁₆" (5mm) dia.
- Screw eye: ⅛" (3mm)

- Tape, hot glue, or wire brads for stacking (see page 8)
- Painter's tape and spray adhesive for attaching patterns
- Wood glue
- Sandpaper
- Finish: See page 7 for suggestions

Tools

- Scroll saw and blades
- Drill and bits: #43 (or size to match toothpick); ⁷⁄₆₄"(3mm); ⁹⁄₆₄"(3.5mm); ¹¹⁄₆₄" (4mm); ³⁄₁₆" (5mm)
- Clamps

CONSTRUCTION NOTES

1. Attach the patterns and cut the pieces. The base (A) and hub (D) are both sloped; the turret (B) has one angled face. You can stack-cut the blades (H) and roof pieces (I); leave the roof pieces slightly oversized so you can custom-fit them.

2. Insert the turret axle (C) through the hole in the top of the turret and into the base. The nail should fit tightly into the base but be loose enough for the turret to spin.

3. Attach the hub to the turret with the hub peg (E); trim peg length as needed. Attach the tail (F) to the turret with a toothpick (G) cut to length. Glue the blades to the hub.

4. Dry-fit the roof pieces to the top of the turret with the angled edges flush with the front and an overhang at the back. Sand an angle into the pieces or cut them to fit as needed. Drill a pilot hole and insert a ⅛" (3mm) screw eye in the center top for hanging.

PARTS LIST

PART	NAME	QTY	MATERIAL	DIMENSIONS
A	Base	1	1⅛" (2.9cm) thick	Pattern
B	Turret	1	¾" (1.9cm) thick	Pattern
C	Turret axle	1	6d box nail	
D	Hub	1	¼" (3mm) thick	Pattern
E	Hub peg	1	³⁄₁₆" (5mm)-dia. axle peg	Purchased

PART	NAME	QTY	MATERIAL	DIMENSIONS
F	Tail	1	³⁄₁₆" (5mm) thick	Pattern
G	Tail peg	1	Toothpick	
H	Blades	4	¹⁄₁₆" (2mm) thick	Pattern
I	Roof	2	¹⁄₁₆" (2mm) thick	Pattern

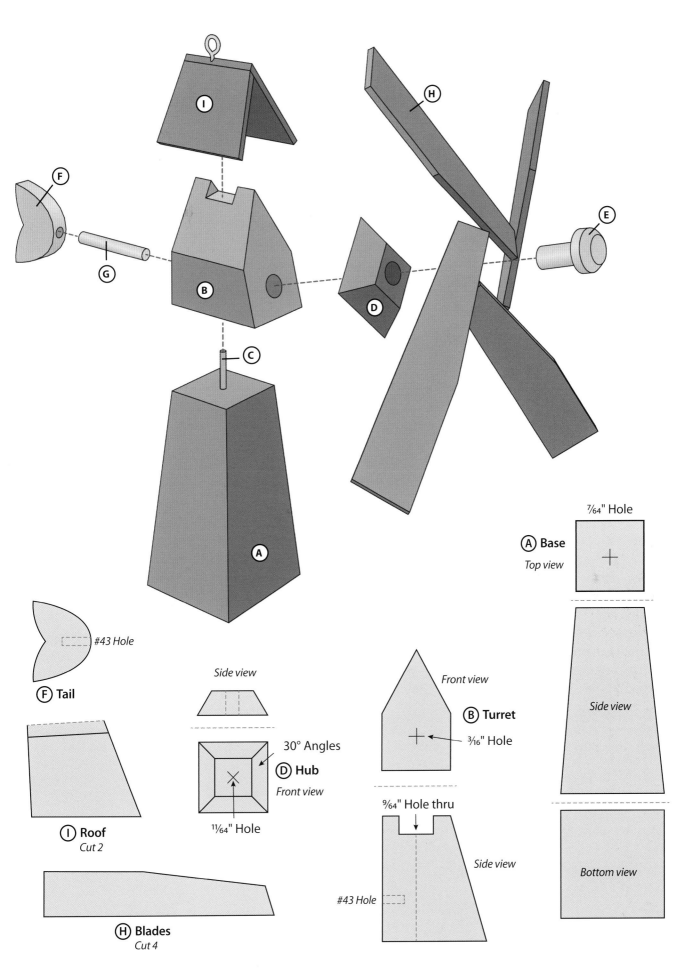

(F) **Tail**

#43 Hole

(I) **Roof**
Cut 2

(H) **Blades**
Cut 4

Side view

30° Angles

(D) **Hub**
Front view

¹¹⁄₆₄" Hole

Front view

(B) **Turret**

³⁄₁₆" Hole

⁹⁄₆₄" Hole thru

Side view

#43 Hole

⁷⁄₆₄" Hole

(A) **Base**

Top view

Side view

Bottom view

WINDMILL 27

TRACTOR

Materials

- Scrap wood:
  ¾" (1.9cm) thick
  ⅝" (1.6cm) thick
  ⁷⁄₁₆" (1.1cm) thick
  ¼" (6mm) thick
  ³⁄₁₆" (5mm) thick
  ⅛" (3mm) thick
- Dowel: ¼" (6mm)
  dia.; ³⁄₁₆" (5mm) dia.;
  ⅛" (3mm) dia.;
  ⅜" (10mm) (optional—
  see steering wheel)
- Toothpicks: round wooden

- Wooden wheels: 2 each
  ½" (1.3cm) dia.; 2 each
  1¼" (3.2cm) dia.
- Screw eye: ⅛" (3mm)
- Painter's tape and
  spray adhesive for
  attaching patterns
- Wood glue
- Sandpaper
- Acrylic paint (optional)
- Finish: See page 7
  for suggestions

Tools

- Scroll saw and blades
- Drill and bits: #43 (or size
  to match toothpicks);

  ³⁄₁₆" (5mm); ⁹⁄₆₄" (3.5mm);
  ¹⁷⁄₆₄" (3mm)
- Clamps

CONSTRUCTION NOTES

1. Attach the patterns, drill the holes, and cut the pieces. Cut the sides and back only of the base (A), radiator (B), and hood (D); leave the pattern on the hood. Glue the base, radiator, hood, and divider (C) together and let dry. Then, cut the front curve of the assembly. Cut five evenly spaced slots about ¼" (6mm) deep in the front of the radiator. Bevel the top edges of the hood.

2. Assemble the steering wheel (F, G) and glue it into the divider. Glue the rear axle block (H) around the base about ³⁄₁₆" (5mm) from the back. Drill the axle hole through the assembly. Glue one rear wheel (I) to the rear axle (J), slide the axle through the hole in the block, and glue the second wheel to the axle.

3. Drill a ⁹⁄₆₄" (3.5mm)-dia. hole about ⅛" (3mm) from the end of the front wheel pin (K). Trim the pin to 1¼" (3.2cm) long. Glue one front wheel (L) to the front axle (M), slide the axle through the hole in the pin, and glue the second wheel to the axle. Dry-fit the pin into the hole in the front of the base, cut the pin so the front and back wheels are equal in height, and glue the pin in place.

4. Glue the exhaust pipe (E) in place. Glue the seat (O) to the seat bracket (N) and paint the assembly if desired. Glue it to the base. Drill a pilot hole and insert a ⅛" (3mm) screw eye in the hood for hanging.

PARTS LIST

PART	NAME	QTY	MATERIAL	DIMENSIONS
A	Base	1	¼" (6mm) thick	Pattern
B	Radiator	1	¾" (1.9cm) thick	Pattern
C	Divider	1	⅛" (3mm) thick	Pattern
D	Hood	1	³⁄₁₆" (5mm) thick	Pattern
E	Exhaust pipe	1	³⁄₁₆" (5mm)-dia. dowel	1½" (3.8cm) long
F	Steering wheel	1	⅛" (3mm) thick OR ⅜" (10mm)-dia. dowel	Use pattern on wood OR cut ⅛" (3mm) length of dowel
G	Steering wheel shaft	1	Toothpick	¾" (1.9cm) long
H	Rear axle block	1	⁷⁄₁₆" (1.1cm) thick	Pattern; do not drill hole yet

PART	NAME	QTY	MATERIAL	DIMENSIONS
I	Rear wheels	2	1¼" (3.2cm) dia.	Purchased
J	Rear axle	1	¼" (6mm)-dia. dowel	1⅞" (4.8cm) long
K	Front wheel pin	1	³⁄₁₆" (5mm)-dia. dowel	3" (7.6cm) long (oversized blank)
L	Front wheels	2	½" (1.3cm) dia.	Purchased
M	Front axle	1	⅛" (3mm)-dia. dowel	⅝" (1.6cm) long
N	Seat bracket	1	⅝" (1.6cm) thick	Pattern
O	Seat	1	⅛" (3mm) thick	Pattern

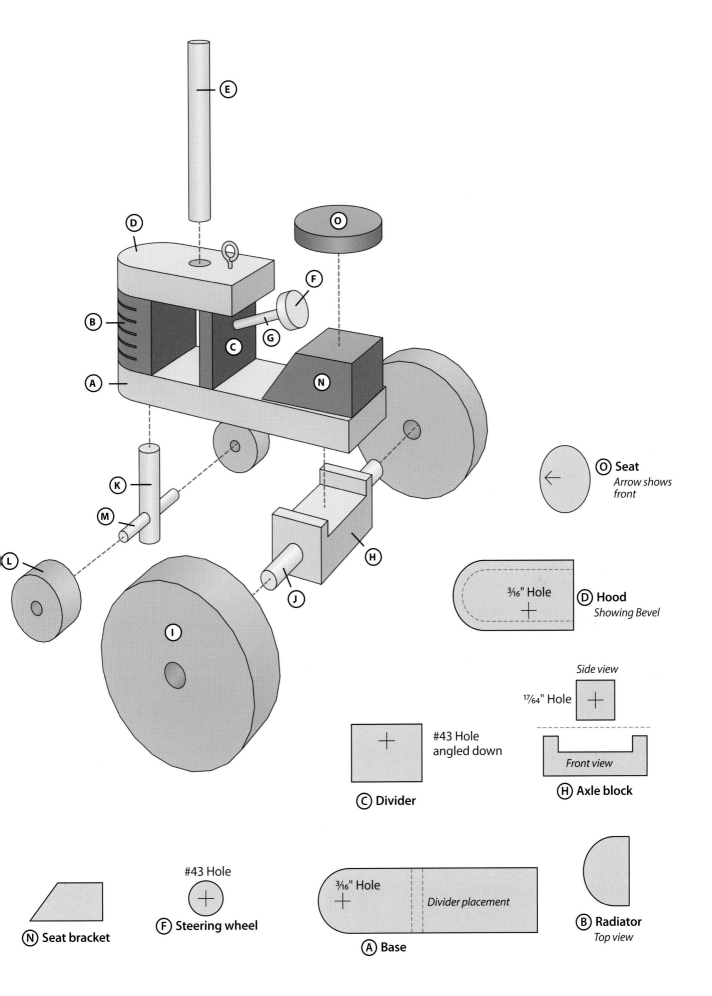

E

D

O Seat
Arrow shows front

B

F

C

G

N

³⁄₁₆" Hole D Hood
Showing Bevel

K

M

Side view

¹⁷⁄₆₄" Hole

L

#43 Hole
angled down

Front view

J

C Divider

H Axle block

I

N Seat bracket

#43 Hole

F Steering wheel

³⁄₁₆" Hole

Divider placement

A Base

B Radiator
Top view

WAGON

Materials

- Scrap wood:
  3⁄16" (5mm) thick
  1⁄8" (3mm) thick
  1⁄16" (2mm) thick
- Dowel: 3⁄16" (5mm) dia.; 1⁄8" (3mm) dia.
- Wooden wheels: 4 each 3⁄4" (1.9cm) dia.
- Axle peg: 1⁄8" (3mm) dia.
- Screw eye: 1⁄8" (3mm)
- Tape, hot glue, or wire brads for stacking (see page 8)
- Painter's tape and spray adhesive for attaching patterns
- Wood glue
- Sandpaper
- Finish: See page 7 for suggestions

Tools

- Scroll saw and blades
- Drill and bits: 1⁄8" (3mm); 9⁄64" (3.5mm); 3⁄16" (5mm); 1⁄4" (6mm)
- Clamps

CONSTRUCTION NOTES

1. Attach the patterns, drill the holes, and cut the pieces. You can stack-cut the front/back (B), sides (C), and axle blocks (D, E) (see page 8 for instructions). Sand a taper into the back outside half of both front axle blocks (E).
2. Glue the back axle blocks (D) to the underside of the bottom (A). Glue the front/back (B) between the sides (C) on the top side of the bottom piece, aligned with the front of the wagon.
3. Glue the front axle blocks (E) to the edges of the steering block (F) with the backs of the pieces aligned and the tapered side of each axle block on the outside. Slide the handle axle (H) through the handle (G). Align the handle with the notch in the steering block and glue the axle to the front of the block; don't get glue on the handle.
4. Position the steering assembly under the wagon bottom. Insert the steering axle (K) through the hole in the wagon bottom and glue it into the steering assembly; don't get glue on the wagon bottom or the assembly won't turn.
5. Glue one wheel (I) to each axle (J), slide the axle through the holes in the axle blocks, and glue a second wheel to each axle. Drill a pilot hole and insert a 1⁄8" (3mm) screw eye in the wagon for hanging.

PARTS LIST

PART	NAME	QTY	MATERIAL	DIMENSIONS
A	Bottom	1	1⁄8" (3mm) thick	Pattern
B	Front/back	2	1⁄16" (2mm) thick	3⁄8" x 1¼" (5mm x 3.2cm)
C	Sides	2	1⁄16" (2mm) thick	3⁄8" x 2 13⁄16" (5mm x 7.1cm)
D	Back axle blocks	2	1⁄8" (3mm) thick	Pattern
E	Front axle blocks	2	1⁄8" (3mm) thick	Pattern
F	Steering block	1	3⁄16" (5mm) thick	Pattern
G	Handle	1	1⁄8" (3mm) thick	Pattern
H	Handle axle	1	3⁄16" (5mm)-dia. dowel	13⁄16" (3cm) long
I	Wheels	4	3⁄4" (1.9cm)-dia.	Purchased
J	Wheel axle	2	1⁄8" (3mm)-dia. dowel	2" (5.1cm) long
K	Steering axle	1	1⁄8" (3mm)-dia. axle peg	Purchased

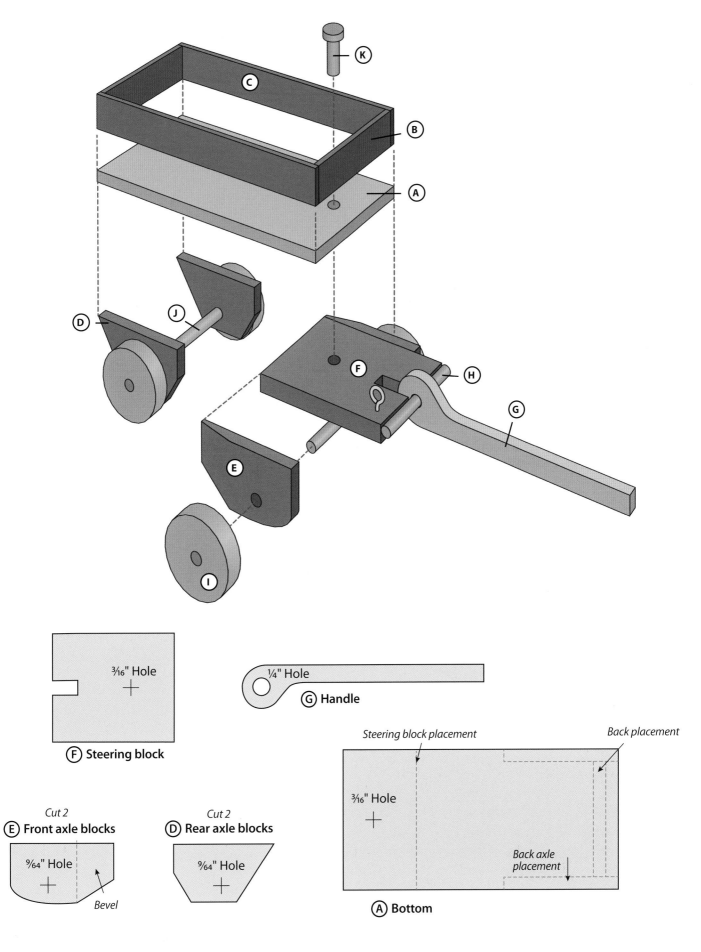

(K)

(C)

(B)

(A)

(D)

(J)

(F)

(H)

(G)

(E)

(I)

¾6" Hole

(F) **Steering block**

¼" Hole

(G) **Handle**

Cut 2
(E) **Front axle blocks**

%4" Hole

Bevel

Cut 2
(D) **Rear axle blocks**

%4" Hole

Steering block placement

Back placement

¾6" Hole

Back axle placement

(A) **Bottom**

TUGBOAT

Materials

- Scrap wood:
  Note: I use maple and walnut to get the contrasting colors.
  5/8" (1.6cm) thick
  1/4" (6mm) thick
  1/16" (2mm) thick
- Dowel: 3/8" (1cm) dia.
- Toothpicks: round wooden
- Screw eye: 1/8" (3mm)

- Tape, hot glue, or wire brads for stacking (see page 8)
- Painter's tape and spray adhesive for attaching patterns
- Wood glue
- Sandpaper
- Acrylic paint
- Finish: See page 7 for suggestions

Tools

- Scroll saw and blades
- Drill and bits: #43 (or size to match toothpicks); 3/8" (1cm) dia.
- Clamps

CONSTRUCTION NOTES

1. Stack the three hull blanks (A) (see page 8 for instructions) and attach the pattern to the top layer. Use a #43 bit to drill the pin holes through the top two layers and into, but not through, the bottom layer. Angle the holes away from the cabin. Drill the smokestack hole through the top layer and into the middle layer.

2. Tilt the saw approximately 15 degrees and cut the boat perimeter. Remove the bottom layer. Cut across the remaining stack just behind the smokestack. Separate the layers. Cut the top, U-shaped layer and sand so it tapers to 1/8" (3mm) thick at ends of the U.

3. Cut and paint the smokestack (D). Cut the cabin (B) and paint square windows on three sides. Cut and glue on the roof, positioning it with the overhang in the front. Drill a pilot hole and insert a 1/8" (3mm) screw eye in the roof for hanging.

4. Dry-fit wooden toothpicks into the four pin holes with 1/4" (6mm) protruding. Align and glue the layers, and then align and glue the cabin and smokestack.

PARTS LIST

PART	NAME	QTY	MATERIAL	DIMENSIONS	PART	NAME	QTY	MATERIAL	DIMENSIONS
A	Hull layers	3	1/4" (6mm) thick	Pattern	D	Smokestack	1	3/8" (1cm)-dia. dowel	1 7/8" (4.8cm) long
B	Cabin	1	5/8" (1.6cm) square	7/8" (2.2cm) tall	E	Hull pins	3	Toothpicks	Cut to fit
C	Roof	1	1/16" (2mm) thick	3/4" x 7/8" (1.9cm x 2.2cm)					

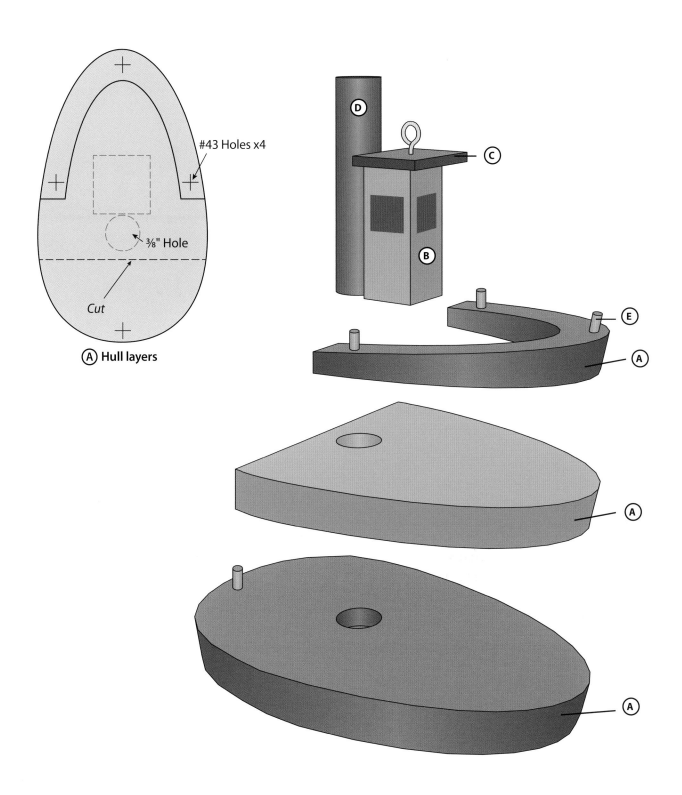

#43 Holes x4

⅜" Hole

Cut

Ⓐ Hull layers

Ⓓ

Ⓒ

Ⓑ

Ⓔ

Ⓐ

Ⓐ

Ⓐ

1909 CADILLAC

Materials
- Scrap wood:
  - ½" (1.3cm) thick
  - ³⁄₁₆" (5mm) thick
  - ¼" (6mm) thick
  - ⅛" (3mm) thick
  - ¹⁄₁₆" (2mm) thick
- Dowel: ⅛" (3mm) dia.
- Wooden wheels: 5 each ½" (1.3cm) dia.
- Screw eye: ⅛" (3mm)
- Tape, hot glue, or wire brads for stacking (see page 8)
- Painter's tape and spray adhesive for attaching patterns
- Wood glue
- Sandpaper
- Finish: See page 7 for suggestions

Tools
- Scroll saw and blades
- Drill and bit: ⁹⁄₆₄" (3.5mm)
- Clamps

CONSTRUCTION NOTES

1. Attach the patterns to the wood, drill the blade-entry holes, and cut the pieces. You can stack-cut the sides (C), fenders (N), and seat pieces (F, G, H, I) (see page 8 for instructions). The rear-seat riser, bottom, and back will be approximately ⅞" (2.2cm) long. The front-seat riser, bottom, and back will be approximately ¹³⁄₁₆" (2cm) long. I suggest you cut slightly oversized pieces and then mark and cut them to fit. Drill a ⁹⁄₆₄" (3.5mm) hole lengthwise through each axle block. Sand the convertible top (O) so it's a scant ⅛" (3mm) thick at the front edges.

2. Glue the back (A) to the floor (B). When it is dry, sand the back flush with the floor. Glue the sides (C) to the floor and sand flush.

3. Mark the seat risers (D, E), cut to fit between the sides and glue in place. Mark and cut the seat backs and bottoms (F, G, H, I), and glue them to the risers.

4. Glue the windshield (K) to the hood (J). Let dry, and then glue the assembly to the chassis. Glue the fenders (N) in place, being sure to place them with the front end forward. Add the convertible top (O), with the tapered side up, and the radiator (P).

5. Align and glue the axle blocks. Glue one wheel (Q) to each axle (R), slide it through an axle block, and dry-fit the other wheel on each axle. Leave ¹⁄₁₆" (2mm) clearance between the chassis and the wheels. Adjust and glue the wheels, and cut the axle flush. Glue a spare tire to the side. Drill a pilot hole and insert a ⅛" (3mm) screw eye for hanging.

PARTS LIST

PART	NAME	QTY	MATERIAL	DIMENSIONS	PART	NAME	QTY	MATERIAL	DIMENSIONS
A	Back	1	⅛" (3mm) thick	Pattern	H	Rear seat bottom	1	¹⁄₁₆" (2mm) thick	⁵⁄₁₆" x 1" (8mm x 2.5cm) (oversize; cut to fit)
B	Floor	1	⅛" (3mm) thick	Pattern	I	Front seat bottom	1	¹⁄₁₆" (2mm) thick	⁵⁄₁₆" x 1" (8mm x 2.5cm) (oversize; cut to fit)
C	Side	2	⅛" (3mm) thick	Pattern	J	Hood	1	½" (1.3cm) thick	Pattern
D	Rear seat riser	1	¼" (6mm) square	1" (2.5cm) (oversize; cut to fit)	K	Windshield	1	¹⁄₁₆" (2mm) thick	Pattern
E	Front seat riser	1	¼" (6mm) square	1" (2.5cm) (oversize; cut to fit)	L	Front axle block	1	¼" (6mm) square	1⅛" (2.9cm) long
F	Rear seat back	1	¹⁄₁₆" (2mm) thick	¼" x 1" (6mm x 2.5cm) (oversize; cut to fit)	M	Rear axle block	1	¼" (6mm) square	1³⁄₁₆" (3cm) long
					N	Fenders	2	³⁄₁₆" (5mm) thick	Pattern
G	Front seat back	1	¹⁄₁₆" (2mm) thick	¼" x 1" (6mm x 2.5cm) (oversize; cut to fit)	O	Convertible top	1	¼" (6mm) thick	Pattern
					P	Radiator	1	¹⁄₁₆" (2mm) thick	Pattern
					Q	Wheels	5	½" (1.3cm) dia.	Purchased
					R	Axles	2	⅛" (3mm)-dia. dowel	1⁷⁄₁₆" (3.6cm) long

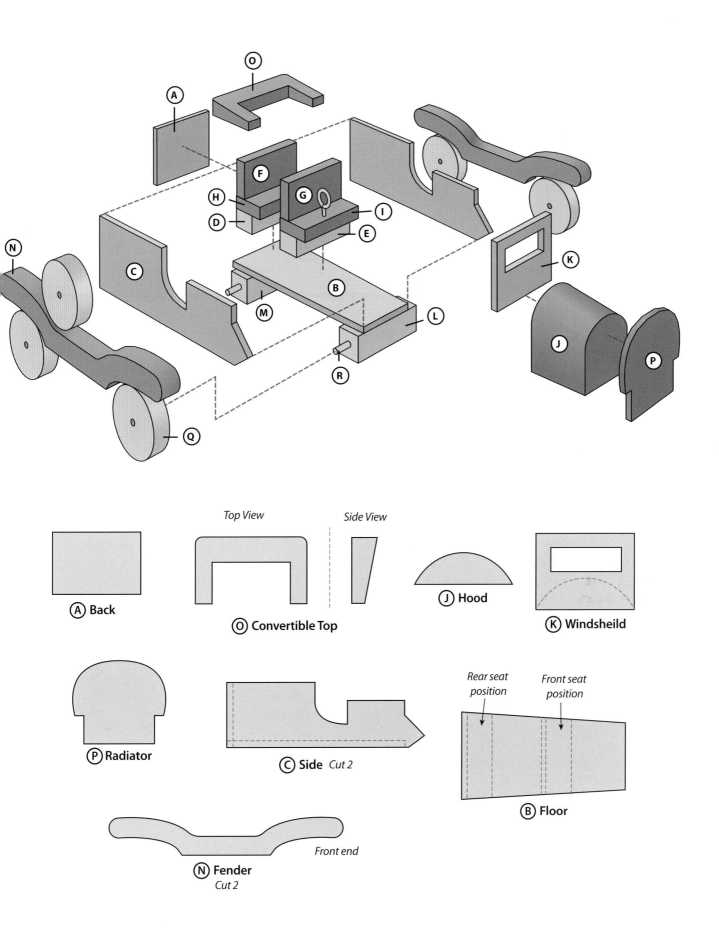

(A) **Back**

Top View

(O) **Convertible Top**

Side View

(J) **Hood**

(K) **Windsheild**

(P) **Radiator**

(C) **Side** *Cut 2*

Rear seat position

Front seat position

(B) **Floor**

Front end

(N) **Fender**
Cut 2

FERRIS WHEEL

Materials
- Scrap wood:
  - ⅝" 1.6cm) thick
  - ⅛" (3mm) thick
  - 1/16" (2mm) thick
- Toothpicks: round wooden
- Screw eye: ⅛" (3mm)
- Tape, hot glue, or wire brads for stacking (see page 8)
- Painter's tape and spray adhesive for attaching patterns
- Wood glue
- Sandpaper
- Finish: See page 7 for suggestions

Tools
- Scroll saw and blades
- Drill and bits: #43 (or size to match toothpicks); 9/64" (3.5mm)
- Clamps

CONSTRUCTION NOTES

1. Attach the patterns, drill the holes (including blade-entry holes), and cut the pieces. You can stack-cut everything except the seats (see page 8 for instructions). Make sure the straight edges of the braces (C) are flat and square.

2. Glue one seat axle (F) into each of the perimeter holes in a wheel (D). Slide a seat (E) onto each axle, being sure they all face the same direction. Align and glue the second wheel, being careful not to get glue on the seats. Let dry.

3. Glue the main axle (G) to one upright (B). Slide the wheel assembly in place and dry-fit the other upright onto the axle. Position the assembly on the base (A), adjust and glue the main axle, trimming excess dowel as needed. Glue the uprights to the base, and glue the braces (C) in place. Drill a pilot hole and insert a ⅛" (3mm) screw eye in an upright for hanging.

PARTS LIST

PART	NAME	QTY	MATERIAL	DIMENSIONS
A	Base	1	⅛" (3mm) thick	1½" x 3⅛" (3.8cm x 7.9cm); see pattern for placement
B	Uprights	2	⅛" (3mm) thick	Pattern
C	Braces	2	⅛" (3mm) thick	Pattern
D	Wheels	1	1/16" (2mm) thick	Pattern
E	Seats	6	⅝" (1.6cm) thick	Pattern; drill before cutting
F	Seat axles	6	Toothpicks	15/16" (2.3cm) long
G	Main axle	1	Toothpicks	1½" (3.8cm)

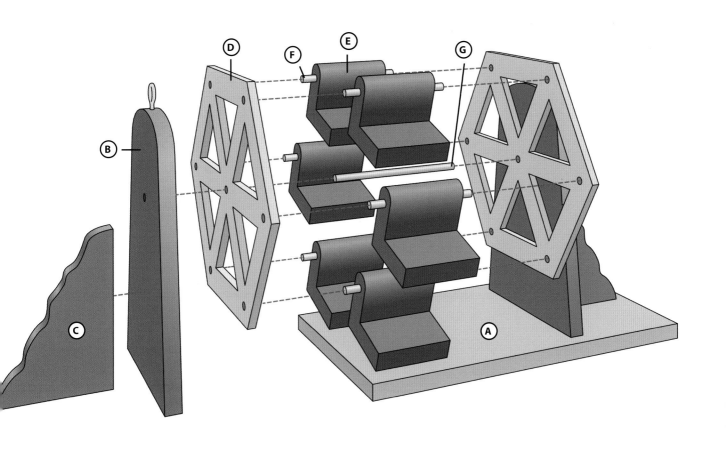

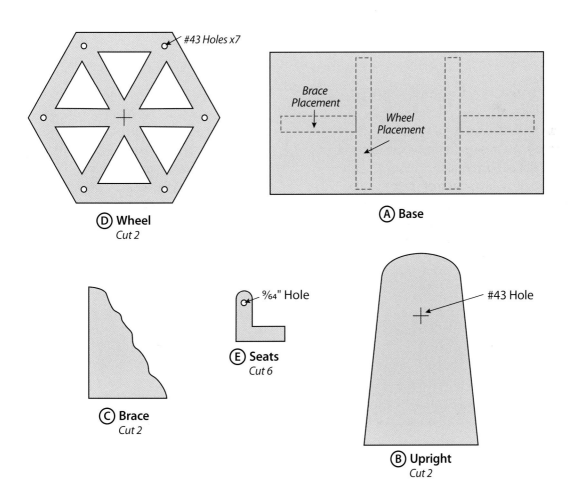

(D) **Wheel**
Cut 2

#43 Holes x7

(A) **Base**

Brace
Placement

Wheel
Placement

(C) **Brace**
Cut 2

(E) **Seats**
Cut 6

⁹⁄₆₄" Hole

(B) **Upright**
Cut 2

#43 Hole

BREAD TRUCK

Materials
- Scrap wood:
  ¾" (1.9cm) thick
  ⅛" (3mm) thick
- Dowel: ⅛" (3mm) dia.
- Wooden wheels: 4 each
  ½" (1.3cm) dia.
- Screw eye: ⅛" (3mm)

- Tape, hot glue, or wire brads for stacking (see page 8)
- Painter's tape and spray adhesive for attaching patterns
- Wood glue
- Sandpaper
- Finish: See page 7 for suggestions

Tools
- Scroll saw and blades
- Drill and bits: #22; ⁹⁄₆₄" (3.5mm)
- Clamps

CONSTRUCTION NOTES

1 Attach the body (A) pattern to the wood, and then drill the holes in the bottom. Stop about ⅛" (3mm) short of drilling through the wood. Drill the axle holes through the sides. Cut the body. Attach the pattern and cut the fenders (B), stack-cutting if desired (see page 8 for instructions).

2 Insert the posts (C) up through the bottom and glue them in place. Cut the dowels flush with the bottom of the truck. Glue a wheel (D) onto each axle (E), slide them through the axle holes, and glue a second wheel to each axle. Glue the fenders in place. Drill a pilot hole and insert a ⅛" (3mm) screw eye for hanging.

PARTS LIST

PART	NAME	QTY	MATERIAL	DIMENSIONS	PART	NAME	QTY	MATERIAL	DIMENSIONS
A	Body	1	¾" (1.9cm) thick	Pattern; drill holes in bottom before cutting	C	Posts	2	⅛" (3mm)-dia. dowel	2" (5.1cm) (oversized)
B	Fenders	2	⅛" (3mm) thick	Pattern	D	Wheels	4	½" (1.3cm) dia.	Purchased
					E	Axles	2	⅛" (3mm)-dia. dowel	1³⁄₁₆" (3.1cm) long

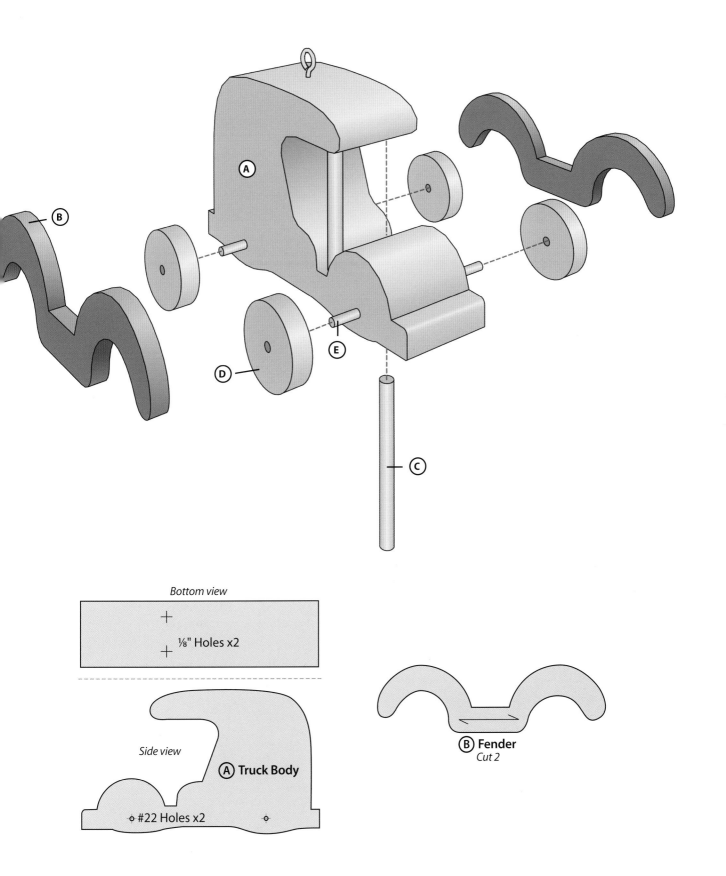

Bottom view

⅛" Holes x2

Side view

Ⓐ **Truck Body**

⊕ #22 Holes x2 ⊕

Ⓑ **Fender**
Cut 2

WISHING WELL

Materials
- Scrap wood:
  ¾" (1.9cm) thick
  ³⁄₁₆" (5mm) thick
  ⅛" (3mm) thick
  ¹⁄₁₆" (2mm) thick
- Dowel: ⅛" (3mm) dia.
- Permanent pen: black OR woodburner with writing tip
- Screw eye: ⅛" (3mm)
- Miniature metal bucket and string (optional)

- Tape, hot glue, or wire brads for stacking (see page 8)
- Painter's tape and spray adhesive for attaching patterns
- Wood glue
- Sandpaper
- Finish: See page 7 for suggestions

Tools
- Scroll saw and blades
- Drill and bits:
  ³⁄₁₆" (5mm);
  1⅝" (4.1cm) Forstner
- Clamps

CONSTRUCTION NOTES

1. Attach the patterns, drill the holes, and cut the pieces. You can stack-cut all of the pieces requiring multiples (see page 8 for instructions). Use a 1⅝" (4.1cm) Forstner bit to drill a ½" (1.3cm)-deep hole in the base (A).

2. Use a permanent pen or woodburner to draw the stone pattern onto the base (see diagram).

3. Glue the roof brackets (B) to the base and glue the roof (C) to the brackets. Glue the handles (E) into the cranks (D). Glue the windlass shaft (F) into the opposite side of one crank, slide it through the roof brackets, and glue the other crank to the shaft. Drill a pilot hole and insert a ⅛" (3mm) screw eye for hanging, making sure it goes into the top of a roof bracket.

If desired, purchase a tiny metal bucket from a craft supply house and tie it to the shaft with a short piece of string.

PARTS LIST

PART	NAME	QTY	MATERIAL	DIMENSIONS
A	Base	1	¾" (1.9cm) thick	Pattern
B	Roof brackets	2	³⁄₁₆" (5mm) thick	Pattern
C	Roof	2	¹⁄₁₆" (2mm) thick	1⅜" x 2⅝" (3.5cm x 6.7cm)

PART	NAME	QTY	MATERIAL	DIMENSIONS
D	Cranks	1	⅛" (3mm) thick	Pattern
E	Crank handles	1	⅛" (3mm)-dia. dowel	½" (1.3cm) long
F	Windlass shaft	1	⅛" (3mm)-dia. dowel	2½" (6.4cm) long

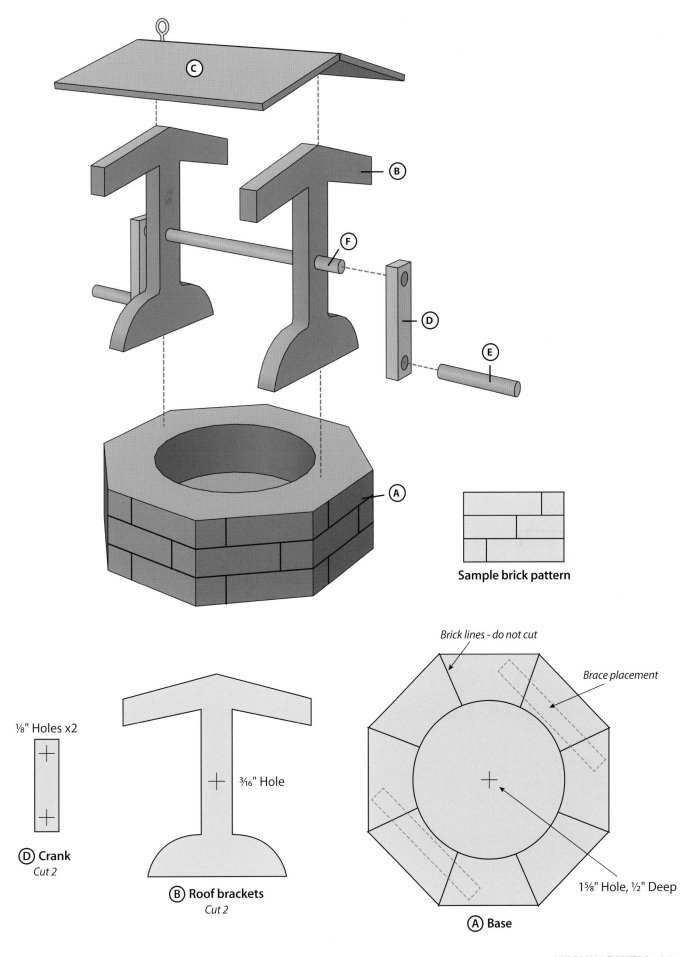

C

B

F

D

E

A

Sample brick pattern

Brick lines - do not cut

Brace placement

⅛" Holes x2

(D) **Crank**
Cut 2

³⁄₁₆" Hole

(B) **Roof brackets**
Cut 2

1⅝" Hole, ½" Deep

(A) **Base**

Materials
- Scrap wood:
  1" (2.5cm) thick
  ⅝" (1.6cm) thick
  1⁄16" (2mm) thick
- Screw eye: ⅛" (3mm)
- Tape, hot glue, or wire brads for stacking (see page 8)
- Painter's tape and spray adhesive for attaching patterns
- Wood glue
- Sandpaper
- Finish: See page 7 for suggestions

Tools
- Scroll saw and blades
- Drill and bits
- Clamps

CONSTRUCTION NOTES

1. Attach the patterns and cut the pieces. You can stack-cut the roof (C) pieces, doors (D), and windows (E). Either cut or sand the center (A) and side (B) sections to a 30-degree angle. Either sand or cut one long edge of each roof piece to a 30-degree angle.

2. Glue the side sections to the center section. Add the roof pieces, doors, and windows. Drill a pilot hole and insert a ⅛" (3mm) screw eye for hanging.

PARTS LIST

PART	NAME	QTY	MATERIAL	DIMENSIONS	PART	NAME	QTY	MATERIAL	DIMENSIONS
A	Center section	1	1" (2.5cm) thick	1½" x 2½" (3.8cm x 6.4cm); see pattern for roof	C	Roof	4	1⁄16" (2mm) thick	⅞" x 3" (2.2cm x 7.6cm)
B	Side sections	2	⅝" (1.6cm) thick	1" x 2½" (2.5cm x 6.4cm); see pattern for roof	D	Doors	2	1⁄16" (2mm) thick	Pattern
					E	Windows	8	1⁄16" (2mm) thick	7⁄16" (1.1cm) square

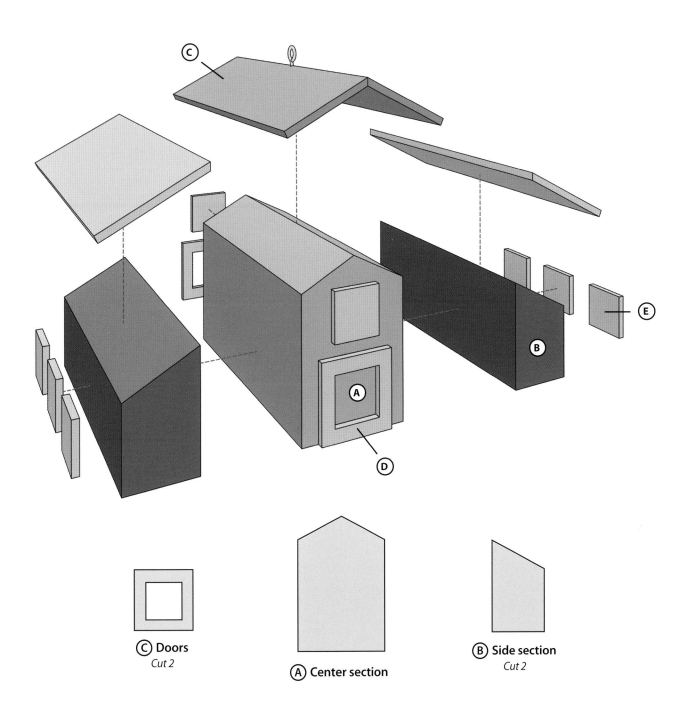

Ⓒ **Doors**
Cut 2

Ⓐ **Center section**

Ⓑ **Side section**
Cut 2

HORSELESS CARRIAGE

Materials
- Scrap wood:
  ½" (1.3cm) thick
  ⅛" (3mm) thick
  1⁄16" (2mm) thick
- Screw eye: ⅛" (3mm)
- Tape, hot glue, or wire brads for stacking (see page 8)

- Painter's tape and spray adhesive for attaching patterns
- Wood glue
- Sandpaper
- Finish: See page 7 for suggestions

Tools
- Scroll saw and blades
- Drill and bits
  9⁄64" (3.5 mm) and
  ¼" (6 mm) drill bits
- Clamps

CONSTRUCTION NOTES

1. Stack the blanks for the chassis center (A) and sides (B) with the center on top (see page 8 for stacking instructions). Attach the pattern to the center, drill the holes, and cut the pieces. Separate the stack, leaving the pattern attached to the center. Cut along the dotted lines. Stack, drill, and cut the remaining pieces. Cut the roof sides (C) slightly oversized.

2. Glue the chassis sides to the center. Add the seat (F).

3. Glue the roof sides (C) to the roof spacer (D). Let dry. Sand the tops of the roof sides flush to fit the spacer. Glue the roof sides to the chassis.

4. Glue a wheel (G) to each axle (H), slide the axles through the holes, and glue another wheel to each axle. Glue the fenders (E) in place, making sure the wheels can spin freely. Drill a pilot hole and insert a ⅛" (3mm) screw eye for hanging.

PARTS LIST

PART	NAME	QTY	MATERIAL	DIMENSIONS
A	Chassis center	1	½" (1.3cm) thick	Pattern
B	Chassis sides	2	⅛" (3mm) thick	Pattern
C	Roof sides	2	1⁄16" (2mm) thick	Pattern; cut slightly oversized
D	Roof spacer	1	½" (1.3cm)	Pattern

PART	NAME	QTY	MATERIAL	DIMENSIONS
E	Fenders	4	⅛" (3mm) thick	Pattern
F	Seat	1	1⁄16" (2mm) thick	¾" x 9⁄16" (1.9cm x 1.4cm)
G	Wheels	4	½" (1.3cm) dia.	Purchased
H	Axles	2	⅛" (3mm)-dia. dowel	1 3⁄16" (3cm) long

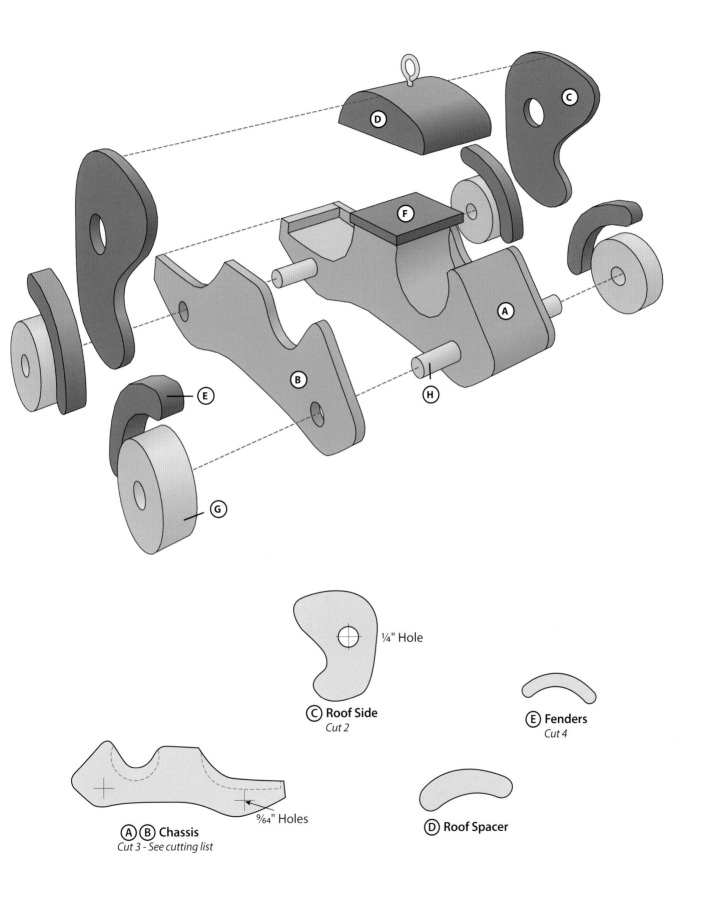

Ⓒ **Roof Side**
Cut 2

¼" Hole

Ⓔ **Fenders**
Cut 4

Ⓐ Ⓑ **Chassis**
Cut 3 - See cutting list

⁹⁄₆₄" Holes

Ⓓ **Roof Spacer**

ADHESIVES

- Wood glue: Choose a good-quality brand, such as Titebond®, Elmer's®, or Gorilla®. They are all available at home-improvement stores.
- Spray adhesive (temporary bond): 3M Spray Mount Repositionable Adhesive is available at craft stores.
- Glue stick: Scotch® Restickable Glue Stick is available at office supply stores.
- Painter's tape: 3M ScotchBlue™ Painter's Tape is available at home-improvement stores.
- Shelf paper: Con-Tact® Brand Adhesive Covering is available at home-improvement and craft stores.

FINISH

All of these finish options are available at home-improvement stores.

- Danish oil: A mixture of tung oil and varnish, Danish oil will sink into the wood. Although it is clear, it will impart a slight yellow color to the wood. Watco Danish oil by Rust-oleum is easy to find.
- Boiled linseed oil: Made from flax oil, boiled linseed oil will slightly yellow over time and creates a slight sheen. It's best used as a basecoat with another finish, such as lacquer spray, over the top. Rags and paper towels used to apply boiled linseed oil can spontaneously combust. Lay them out flat to dry and dispose of them in a metal container. Klean-Strip brand is widely available.
- Lacquer or acrylic spray: These sprays will create a durable topcoat on a project. Krylon and Rust-oleum both make assorted, widely available clear sprays in a variety of sheens.

SCROLL SAW BLADES

If your saw takes pin-end blades, you should be able to find them at home-improvement stores like Home Depot and Lowes.

For plain-end blades, you will probably need to visit a specialty store or shop online. Olson (www.olsonsaw.net) makes a wide variety of blades. Mike's Workshop (mikesworkshop.com) also carries a good assortment of plain-end blades.

WIRE-SIZE DRILL BITS

Although you may not find wire-size bits at a home-improvement store, a local hardware store, such as True Value or Ace Hardware, will often carry them. Or, you can order online from McMaster (www.mcmaster.com) or Gyros (www.gyrostools.com).

CLAMPS

Inexpensive lightweight clamps, such as those carried by Harbor Freight (www.harborfreight.com or 800-423-2567), work fine.

FURTHER INFORMATION

For more sources, scrolling project advice, patterns, and more, visit *Scroll Saw Woodworking & Crafts magazine* online at *www.scrollsawer.com* and look for the magazine at newsstands.

MEET THE AUTHOR

Howard Clements learned the basics of woodworking from his father and grandfather more than 70 years ago. Over the years his projects have ranged from a 2" (5.2cm) spider to a steeple he built for an area church and a cupola for a friend's garage. He has won numerous awards, ribbons, and recognition for his woodworking projects. He creates most of his projects without using a pattern, but if he does use one, he always changes something to make it uniquely his project.

When his grandchildren began arriving more than 30 years ago, Howard started designing and scrolling tiny wooden toy ornaments. He has created nearly two dozen designs. Each Christmas he gives many ornaments as gifts to family and friends. He also uses the scroll saw to make models used in lawsuits and in the courtroom.

Howard displays his creations in large, glass, enclosed cases on the second floor of his woodshop. Many people have visited his display over the years; kids call it the "museum."

Born and raised in the Knox, Pennsylvania, area, Howard continues to live there today with his wife, Georgia, and his dog, Lucy.

NELSON CO. PUBLIC LIBRARY
201 Cathedral Manor
Bardstown, KY 40004-1205